Book & CD for B♭, E♭, Bass Clef and C instruments

VOLUME
10

PLAY 8 SONGS WITH A PROFESSIONAL BAND

HOW TO USE THE CD:

Each song has <u>two</u> tracks:

1) Full Stereo Mix

All recorded instruments are present on this track.

2) Split Track

Piano and **Bass** parts can be removed
by turning down the volume on the LEFT channel.

Guitar, Harmonica, and **Horn** parts can be removed
by turning down the volume on the RIGHT channel.

ISBN 978-1-4234-8708-1

7777 W. BLUEMOUND RD. P.O. BOX 13819 MILWAUKEE, WI 53213

Visit Hal Leonard Online at
www.halleonard.com

CROSS ROAD BLUES
(Crossroads)

Words and Music by
Robert Johnson

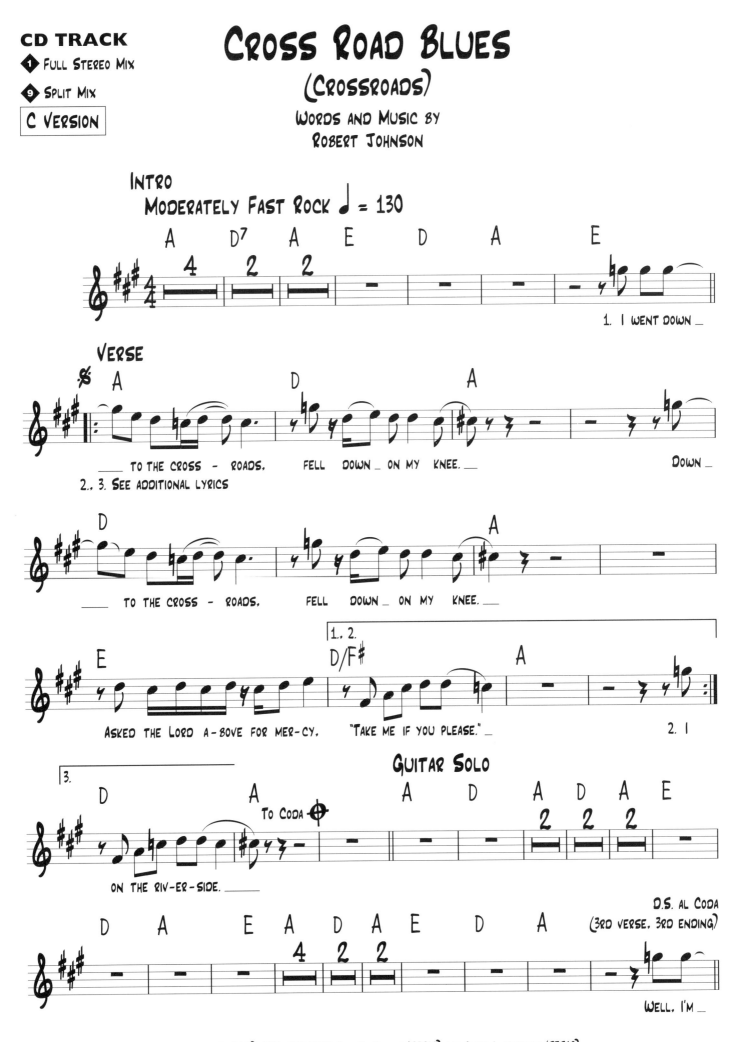

GUITAR SOLO

OUTRO-VERSE

CAN RUN, YOU CAN RUN, TELL MY FRIEND, BOY, WIL-LIE BROWN.

RUN ___ YOU CAN RUN. ___ TELL MY ___ FRIEND BOY, WIL-LIE BROWN. ___

AND I'M STAND-IN' AT THE CROSS - ROAD, BE-

FREE TIME

LIEVE I'M ___ SINK - IN' DOWN.

ADDITIONAL LYRICS

2. I WENT DOWN TO THE CROSSROAD, TRIED TO FLAG A RIDE.
   DOWN TO THE CROSSROAD, TRIED TO FLAG A RIDE.
   NOBODY SEEMED TO KNOW ME; EV'RYBODY PASSED ME BY.

3. WELL, I'M GOIN' DOWN TO ROSEDALE, TAKE MY RIDER BY MY SIDE.
   GOIN' DOWN TO ROSEDALE, TAKE MY RIDER BY MY SIDE.
   WE CAN STILL BARREL HOUSE BABY, ON THE RIVER SIDE.

Give Me Back My Wig

Words and Music by
Theodore "Hound Dog" Taylor

Got My Mo Jo Working

Words and Music by
Preston Foster

ADDITIONAL LYRICS

2. Going down in Louisiana to get me a mojo hand.
Going down in Louisiana to get me a mojo hand.
I'm gonna have all you women; get you under my command.

3. Harp Solo

4. I got a gypsy woman giving me advice.
Got a gypsy woman giving me advice.
I've got a whole lots of tricks keeping here on ice.

THE HOUSE IS ROCKIN'

WRITTEN BY STEVIE RAY VAUGHAN
AND DOYLE BRAMHALL

C Version

PAYING THE COST TO BE THE BOSS

WORDS AND MUSIC BY
B.B. KING

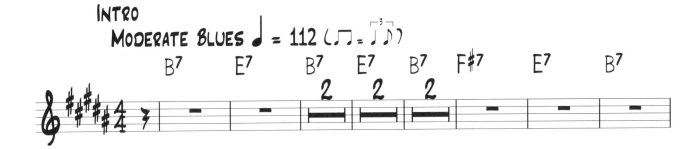

INTRO
MODERATE BLUES ♩ = 112

Lyrics:

1. You act like you don't wan-na lis-ten when I'm talk-in' to you. __ You think you ough-ta do, ba-by, an-y-thing you __ wan-na __ do. _____ You must be cra-zy ba-by, you just got-ta be _____ out of your mind. __ As ___ long as I'm pay-in' the bills. __ wom-an, I'm pay-in' the cost _____ to be the boss. __

2. I'll drink if I wan-na, and play a lit-tle pok-er too.

3. Now that you got me, you act like you're a-shamed.

Don't you say noth-ing to me
You don't act like my wom-an.

As long as I'm tak-in' care of you.
You're just us-in' my name.

As long as I'm work-in', ba - by,
I tell ya I'm gon-na han-dle all the mon-ey

and pay-in' all the bills
and I don't want no back talk.

I don't want no mouth from you
'cause if you don't like the way I'm

a-bout the way I'm sup-posed to
do-in', just pick up your things and

E7

LIVE. You must be cra - zy wom-an,
WALK. You got-ta be cra - zy ba - by,

B7   **F#7**

JUST got-ta be out of your mind.
OH, you must be out of your mind.

As long as I'm foot-in' the bill,
As long as I'm pay-in' the bills.

E7   To Coda ⊕   **B7**   **F#7**

I'm pay-in' the cost to be the boss.
I'm pay-in' the cost to be the

GUITAR SOLO

B7   **E7**   **B7** 2 **E7** 2 **B7** 2 **F#7**   **E7**

D.S. AL CODA

B7   **F#7**

FREE TIME

⊕ **CODA**   **B7**   **B7**

BOSS.

13

Rollin' and Tumblin'

Written by McKinley Morganfield
(Muddy Waters)

MM. MM. _____ MM. MM. _____

MM. _____ MM. MM. MM. ___

___ MM. MM. _____ 4. WELL, IF THE

**VERSE**

RIV-ER WAS WHIS-KEY, _____ AND I WAS A DIV-IN' DUCK. _____
COULD A HAD A RE-LI-GION, _____ THIS BAD OLD THING IN-STEAD. _____

WELL, IF THE RIV-ER WAS WHIS-KEY, _____ AND I WAS A DIV-IN' DUCK. __
WELL, I COULD A HAD A RE-LI-GION, _____ THIS BAD OLD THING IN-STEAD. __

WELL, I WOULD DIVE TO THE __ BOT-TOM.
WELL, NOW __ WHIS-KEY AND WOM-EN

NEV-ER WOULD I __ COME UP. _____ 5. WELL, I
WOULD NOT __ LET _ ME PRAY. __

Turn on Your Love Light

Words and Music by Don Robey and Joe Scott

17

You Can't Judge a Book By the Cover

Written by Willie Dixon

CAN'T JUDGE A BOOK BY LOOK - IN' AT THE

Chorus

COV - ER. WHOA. CAN'T YOU SEE? _____

WHOA. _____ YOU MIS - JUDGED

ME. I

LOOK _____ LIKE A FARM - ER, BUT I'M A LOV - ER.

CAN'T _____ JUDGE A BOOK BY

LOOK - IN' AT THE COV - ER. OH.

1.
Interlude
26
2. YOU

2.
Interlude
14
3. YOU

3.
Outro
16

Cross Road Blues
(Crossroads)

Words and Music by
Robert Johnson

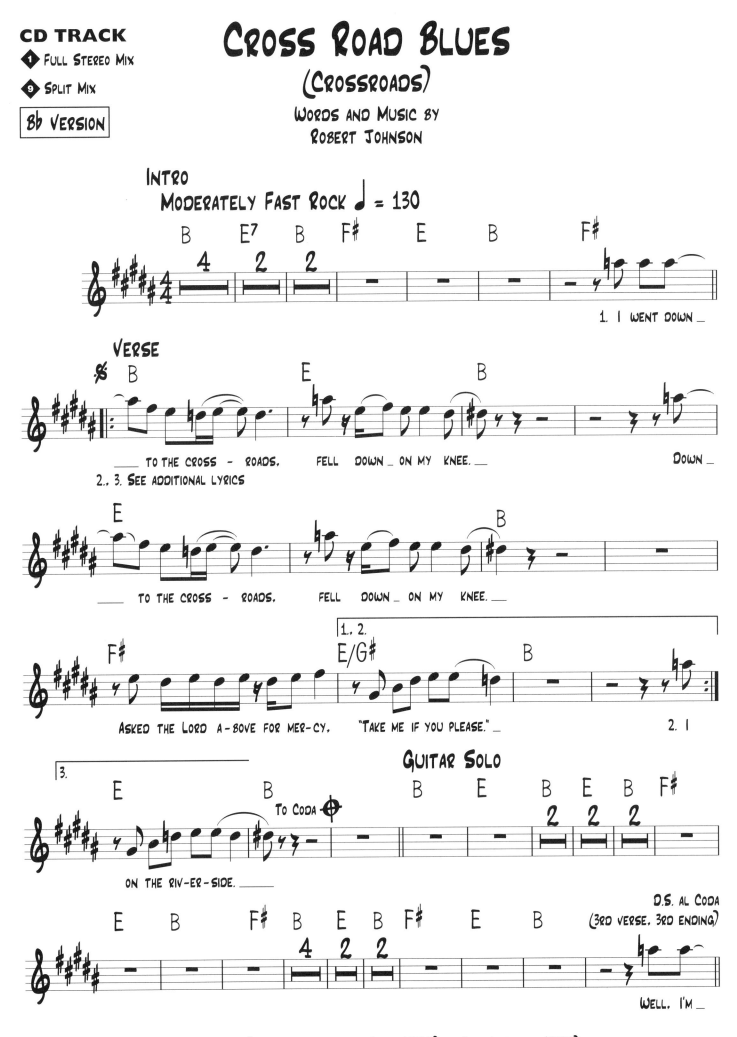

Additional Lyrics

2. I went down to the crossroad, tried to flag a ride.
   Down to the crossroad, tried to flag a ride.
   Nobody seemed to know me; ev'rybody passed me by.

3. Well, I'm goin' down to Rosedale, take my rider by my side.
   Goin' down to Rosedale, take my rider by my side.
   We can still barrel house baby, on the river side.

Give Me Back My Wig

Words and Music by
Theodore "Hound Dog" Taylor

Got My Mo Jo Working

Words and Music by
Preston Foster

Additional Lyrics

2. Going down in Louisiana to get me a mojo hand.
   Going down in Louisiana to get me a mojo hand.
   I'm gonna have all you women; get you under my command.

3. Harp Solo

4. I got a gypsy woman giving me advice.
   Got a gypsy woman giving me advice.
   I've got a whole lots of tricks keeping here on ice.

CD TRACK

4 Full Stereo Mix

12 Split Mix

Bb Version

The House Is Rockin'

Written by Stevie Ray Vaughan
and Doyle Bramhall

ROOM ON THE FLOOR.____ COME ___ ON BA - BY SHAKE SUMP-IN' LOOSE! __
OUT ON THE FLOOR.____ SHIM - MY 'TIL YOU SHAKE SUMP-IN' LOOSE! __

CHORUS

WELL, THE HOUSE ___ IS A-ROCK-IN', DON'T ___ BOTH - ER KNOCK-IN'. WELL, THE

HOUSE ___ IS A-ROCK-IN', DON'T ___ BOTH - ER KNOCK-IN'. WELL, THE HOUSE IS A-ROCK-IN', DON'T ___

_____ BOTH - ER, COME ON ___ IN. ____

PIANO SOLO

GUITAR SOLO

D.S. AL CODA

WELL. __ THE

CODA

I SAID THE HOUSE IS A-ROCK-IN' DON'T __

_____ BOTH-ER, COME ON ___ IN. ____

Paying the Cost to Be the Boss

Words and Music by
B.B. King

INTRO
MODERATE BLUES ♩ = 112

VERSE

1. You act like you don't wan-na lis-ten when I'm talk-in' to you.__ You

think you ough-ta do, ba-by, an-y-thing you __ wan-na __ do. __ You must be cra-zy

ba-by, you just got-ta be _____ out of your mind. __

As __ long as I'm pay-in' the bills. __ Wom-an. I'm pay-in' the cost _____ to be the

VERSE

Boss. __ 2. I'll drink if I wan-na, and play a lit-tle pok-er too.
3. Now that you got me, you act like you're a - shamed.

Rollin' and Tumblin'

Written by McKinley Morganfield
(Muddy Waters)

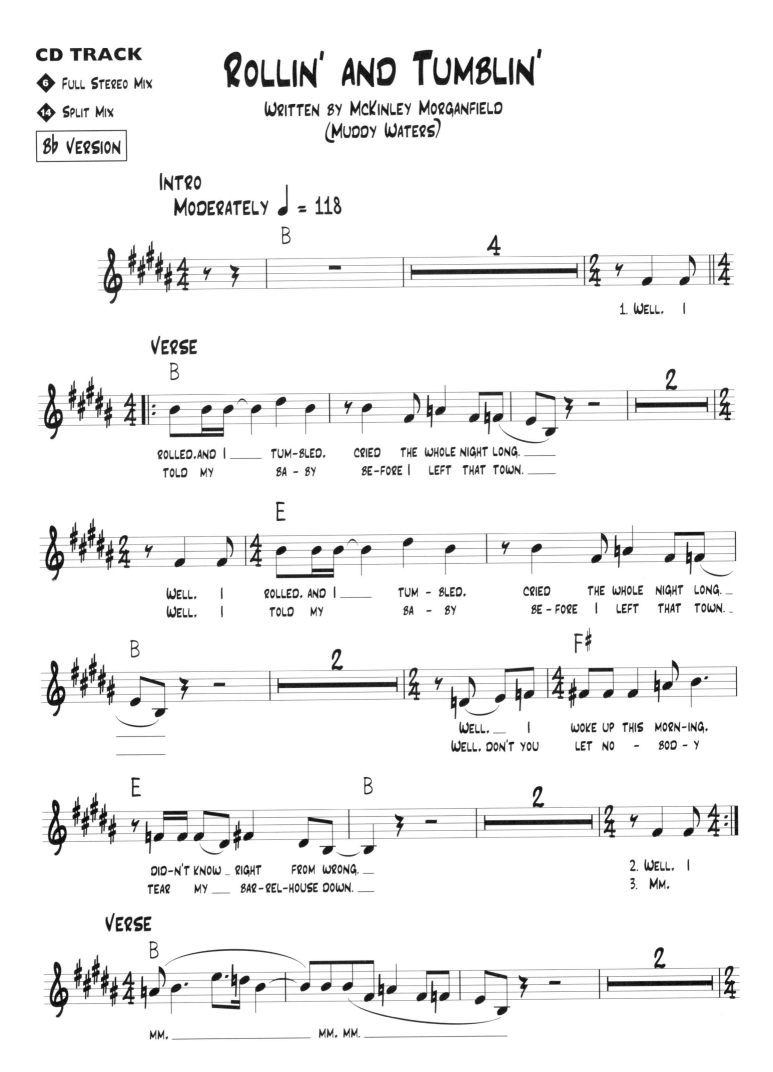

MM, MM, _____ MM, MM. _____

_____ MM, _____ MM, MM, MM, ___

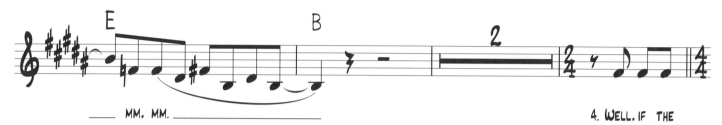

___ MM, MM. _____ 4. WELL, IF THE

Verse

RIV-ER WAS WHIS-KEY, _____ AND I WAS A DIV-IN' DUCK. _____
COULD A HAD A RE-LI-GION, _____ THIS BAD OLD THING IN-STEAD. _____

WELL, IF THE RIV-ER WAS WHIS-KEY, _____ AND I WAS A DIV-IN' DUCK. __
WELL, I COULD A HAD A RE-LI-GION, _____ THIS BAD OLD THING IN-STEAD. _

WELL, I WOULD DIVE TO THE ___ BOT-TOM.
WELL, NOW ___ WHIS-KEY AND WOM-EN

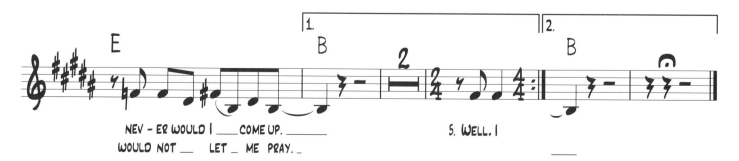

NEV-ER WOULD I ___ COME UP. _____ 5. WELL, I
WOULD NOT ___ LET __ ME PRAY. ___

31

Bb Version

Turn on Your Love Light

Words and Music by Don Robey and Joe Scott

You Can't Judge a Book By the Cover

Written by Willie Dixon

Bb Version

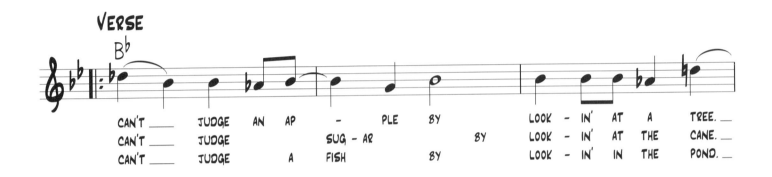

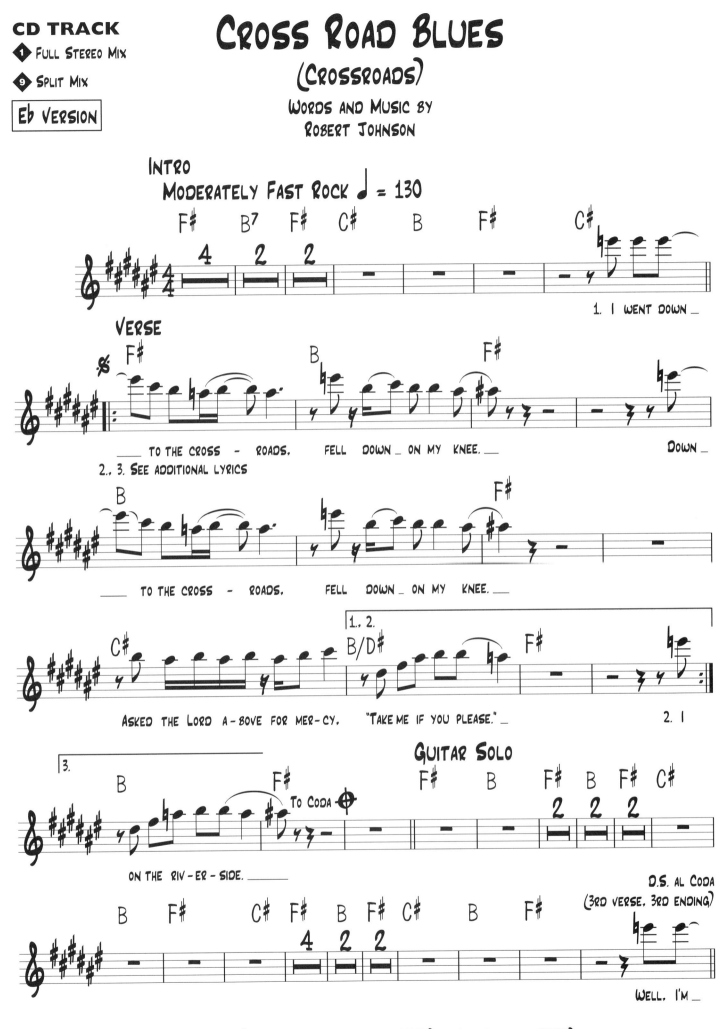

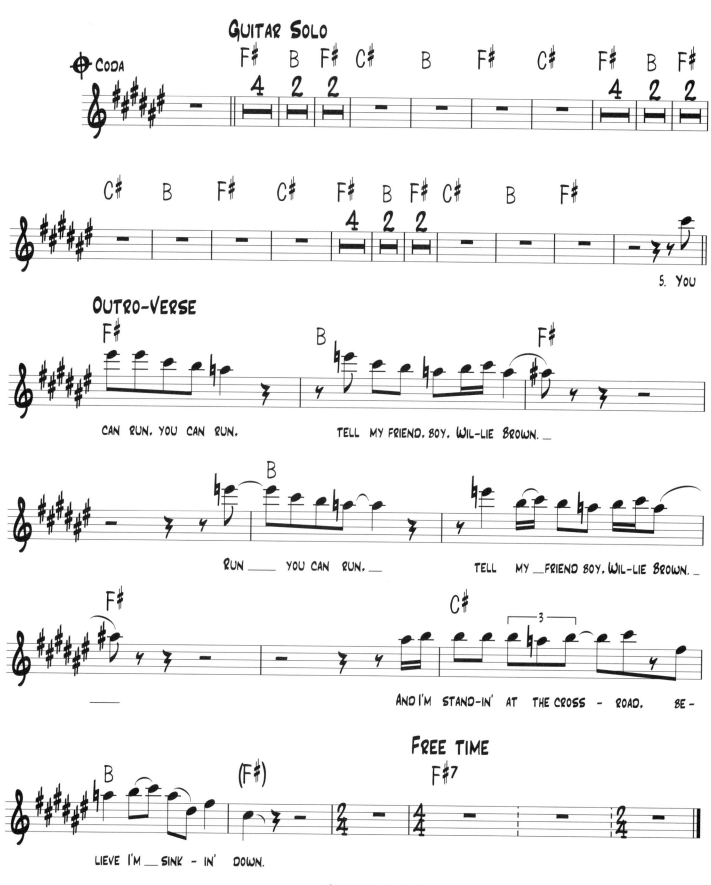

GUITAR SOLO

OUTRO-VERSE

CAN RUN, YOU CAN RUN, TELL MY FRIEND, BOY, WIL-LIE BROWN. __

RUN ___ YOU CAN RUN, __ TELL MY __ FRIEND BOY, WIL-LIE BROWN. __

AND I'M STAND-IN' AT THE CROSS - ROAD, BE-

FREE TIME

LIEVE I'M __ SINK - IN' DOWN.

5. YOU

ADDITIONAL LYRICS

2. I WENT DOWN TO THE CROSSROAD, TRIED TO FLAG A RIDE.
   DOWN TO THE CROSSROAD, TRIED TO FLAG A RIDE.
   NOBODY SEEMED TO KNOW ME; EV'RYBODY PASSED ME BY.

3. WELL, I'M GOIN' DOWN TO ROSEDALE, TAKE MY RIDER BY MY SIDE.
   GOIN' DOWN TO ROSEDALE, TAKE MY RIDER BY MY SIDE.
   WE CAN STILL BARREL HOUSE BABY, ON THE RIVER SIDE.

GIM-ME BACK ___ MY WIG. ___

HON-EY, NOW LET ___ YOUR HEAD ___ GO BALD. ___

REAL-LY DI'N'T HAVE ___ NO BUSI-NESS,

HON-EY, ___ BUY YOU NO WIG ___ AT ALL.

GUITAR SOLO

TO CODA

VERSE

4. GOOD-BYE, LIT - TLE ONE.

ALL I GOT TO SAY.

GIM-ME BACK ___ MY WIG ___ AND BE ON YOUR MER-RY WAY. ___

___ YOU JUST GIM-ME BACK ___ MY WIG. ___

HON-EY, NOW LET ___

___ YOUR HEAD ___ GO BALD. ___

REAL-LY DI'N'T HAVE ___ NO BUSI-NESS,

D.S. AL CODA

HON-EY, ___ BUY YOU NO WIG ___ AT ALL. ___

CODA

Got My Mo Jo Working

Words and Music by
Preston Foster

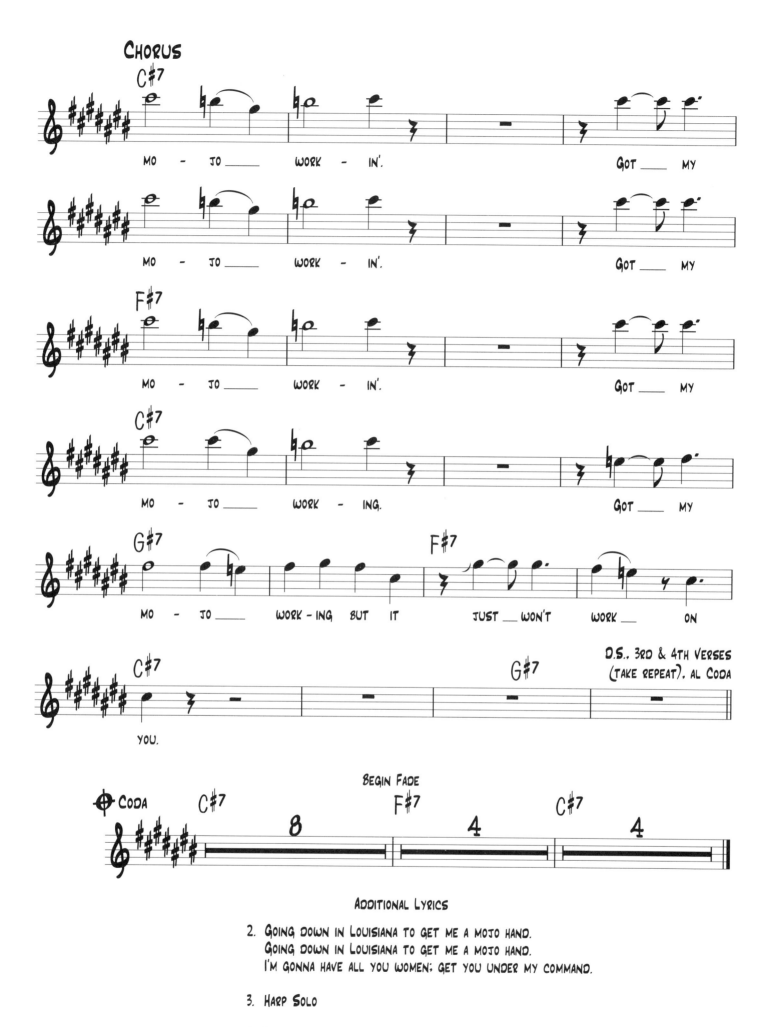

Additional Lyrics

2. Going down in Louisiana to get me a mojo hand.
   Going down in Louisiana to get me a mojo hand.
   I'm gonna have all you women; get you under my command.

3. Harp Solo

4. I got a gypsy woman giving me advice.
   Got a gypsy woman giving me advice.
   I've got a whole lots of tricks keeping here on ice.

Eb Version

The House Is Rockin'
Written by Stevie Ray Vaughan and Doyle Bramhall

ROOM ON THE FLOOR, _____ COME _____ ON BA - BY SHAKE SUMP-IN' LOOSE! _
OUT ON THE FLOOR, _____ SHIM - MY 'TIL YOU SHAKE SUMP-IN' LOOSE! _

CHORUS

WELL, THE HOUSE_ IS A-ROCK-IN', DON'T _ BOTH - ER KNOCK-IN'. WELL, THE

HOUSE _ IS A-ROCK-IN', DON'T _ BOTH - ER KNOCK-IN'. WELL, THE HOUSE IS A-ROCK-IN', DON'T _

To Coda

_____ BOTH - ER, COME ON _____ IN. _____

PIANO SOLO

GUITAR SOLO

D.S. AL CODA

WELL, _ THE

Coda

I SAID THE HOUSE IS A-ROCK-IN' DON'T _

_____ BOTH-ER, COME ON _ IN. _____

43

Don't you say noth-ing to me
You don't act like my wom-an.

As long as I'm tak-in' care of you.
You're just us-in' my name.

As long as I'm work-in', ba - by,
I tell ya I'm gon-na han-dle all the mon-ey

and pay-in' all the bills
and I don't want no back talk,

I don't want no mouth_ from you __
'cause if you don't like the way I'm

a - bout the way I'm ___ sup-posed to
do - in', just pick up your things and

D^b7

live. _____ You must be cra - zy wom-an.
walk. _____ You got - ta be cra - zy ba - by,

A^b7 E^b7

just got-ta be ____ out of your mind. __
oh, you must be out of your mind.

As long as I'm foot-in' the bill,
As long as I'm pay-in' the bills,

D^b7 To Coda ⊕ A^b7 E^b7

I'm pay - in' the cost _____ to be the boss.
I'm pay - in' the cost to be the

Guitar Solo

A^b7 | D^b7 | A^b7 2 | D^b7 2 | A^b7 2 | E^b7 | D^b7

Free Time

A^b7 | E^b7 D.S. al Coda

⊕ Coda A^b7 | A^b7

boss. ____

45

Rollin' and Tumblin'
Written by McKinley Morganfield
(Muddy Waters)

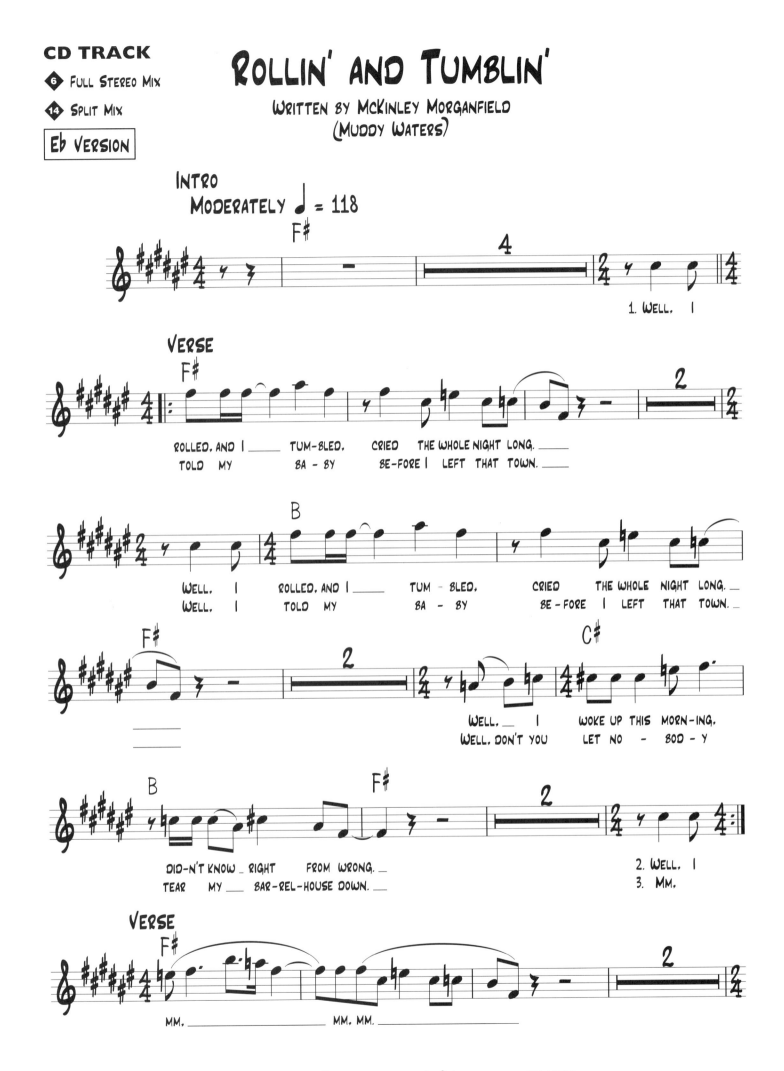

MM. MM. MM. MM.

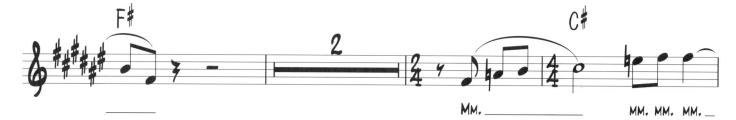

MM. MM. MM. MM.

MM. MM. 4. WELL, IF THE

VERSE

RIV-ER WAS WHIS-KEY,___ AND I WAS A DIV-IN' DUCK.___
COULD A HAD A RE-LI-GION,___ THIS BAD OLD THING IN-STEAD.___

WELL, IF THE RIV-ER WAS WHIS-KEY,___ AND I WAS A DIV-IN' DUCK.__
WELL, I COULD A HAD A RE-LI-GION,___ THIS BAD OLD THING IN-STEAD.__

___ WELL, I WOULD DIVE TO THE ___ BOT-TOM.
___ WELL, NOW ___ WHIS-KEY AND WOM-EN

NEV-ER WOULD I ___ COME UP. ___ 5. WELL, I
WOULD NOT ___ LET ___ ME PRAY. ___

You Can't Judge A Book By The Cover

Written by Willie Dixon

CAN'T JUDGE A BOOK BY LOOK - IN' AT THE

CHORUS

COV - ER. WHOA. CAN'T YOU SEE?

WHOA. YOU MIS - JUDGED

ME.

LOOK LIKE A FARM - ER, BUT I'M A LOV - ER.

CAN'T JUDGE A BOOK BY

LOOK - IN' AT THE COV - ER. OH.

1.
INTERLUDE
F
26

2.
INTERLUDE
F
14

3.
OUTRO
F
16

2. YOU

3. YOU

Cross Road Blues
(Crossroads)

Words and Music by
Robert Johnson

CD TRACK
1 Full Stereo Mix
9 Split Mix

🎼 C Version

Guitar Solo

Outro-Verse

CAN RUN, YOU CAN RUN.   TELL MY FRIEND, BOY, WIL-LIE BROWN. __

RUN ___ YOU CAN RUN, __   TELL MY __ FRIEND BOY, WIL-LIE BROWN. __

___   AND I'M STAND-IN' AT THE CROSS - ROAD.   BE-

Free Time

LIEVE I'M __ SINK - IN' DOWN.

Additional Lyrics

2. I WENT DOWN TO THE CROSSROAD, TRIED TO FLAG A RIDE.
   DOWN TO THE CROSSROAD, TRIED TO FLAG A RIDE.
   NOBODY SEEMED TO KNOW ME; EV'RYBODY PASSED ME BY.

3. WELL, I'M GOIN' DOWN TO ROSEDALE, TAKE MY RIDER BY MY SIDE.
   GOIN' DOWN TO ROSEDALE, TAKE MY RIDER BY MY SIDE.
   WE CAN STILL BARREL HOUSE BABY, ON THE RIVER SIDE.

Give Me Back My Wig

Words and Music by
Theodore "Hound Dog" Taylor

Intro
Fast Swing ♩ = 216

1. GIM-ME BACK __ MY WIG. HON-EY, NOW LET __
___ YOUR HEAD __ GO BALD. ___ GIM-ME BACK __ MY WIG.
HON-EY, NOW LET ___ YOUR HEAD __ GO BALD. ___ REAL-LY DI'N'T HAVE __ NO BUSI-
NESS. HON EY, ___ BUY YOU NO WIG __ AT ALL. ___

Verse

2. TAK-IN' ME ___ DOWN-TOWN, SAY FOUR FOR-TY NINE.
3. YEAH, MY MA-MA TOLD __ ME, TELL YOUR GOOD __ FRIEND TOO.

WHEN I GET __ DOWN THERE, __ I SWEAR, NINE NINE-TY NINE. __ YOU JUST)
WHEN YOU GET __ THAT WIG ___ THAT'S THE WAY YOU'RE GON - NA DO. ___ YOU JUST)

Got My Mo Jo Working

Words and Music by
Preston Foster

Chorus

D.S., 3RD & 4TH VERSES
(TAKE REPEAT), AL CODA

Additional Lyrics

2. Going down in Louisiana to get me a mojo hand.
   Going down in Louisiana to get me a mojo hand.
   I'm gonna have all you women; get you under my command.

3. Harp Solo

4. I got a gypsy woman giving me advice.
   Got a gypsy woman giving me advice.
   I've got a whole lots of tricks keeping here on ice.

The House Is Rockin'

Written by Stevie Ray Vaughan
and Doyle Bramhall

C Version

ROOM ON THE FLOOR. ____ COME ____ ON BA - BY SHAKE SUMP-IN' LOOSE! __
OUT ON THE FLOOR. ____ SHIM - MY 'TIL YOU SHAKE SUMP-IN' LOOSE! __

Chorus

WELL, THE HOUSE_ IS A-ROCK-IN', DON'T _ BOTH - ER KNOCK-IN'. WELL, THE

HOUSE_ IS A-ROCK-IN', DON'T _ BOTH - ER KNOCK-IN'. WELL, THE HOUSE IS A-ROCK-IN'. DON'T _

_____ BOTH - ER, COME ON ____ IN. ____

Piano Solo

Guitar Solo

WELL,_ THE

I SAID THE HOUSE IS A-ROCK-IN' DON'T _

_____ BOTH-ER, COME ON ____ IN. ____

Paying the Cost to Be the Boss

Words and Music by
B.B. King

INTRO
MODERATE BLUES ♩ = 112

B7   E7   B7   E7   B7   F#7   E7   B7
                  2   2   2

VERSE

F#7   B7   E7

1. You act like you don't wan-na lis-ten when I'm talk-in' to you. __ You

B7   E7

think you ough-ta do, ba-by, an-y-thing you __ wan-na __ do. __ You must be cra-zy

B7

ba-by, you just got-ta be __ out of your mind. __

F#7   E7   B7

As __ long as I'm pay-in' the bills, __ wom-an, I'm pay-in' the cost __ to be the

𝄋 VERSE

F#7   B7

boss. __

2. I'll drink if I wan-na, and play a lit-tle pok-er too.
3. Now that you got me, you act like you're a-shamed.

Rollin' And Tumblin'

Written by McKinley Morganfield
(Muddy Waters)

MM, MM, MM, MM.

MM, MM, MM, MM.

MM, MM. 4. WELL, IF THE

VERSE

RIV - ER WAS WHIS - KEY, AND I WAS A DIV - IN' DUCK.
COULD A HAD A RE - LI - GION, THIS BAD OLD THING IN - STEAD.

Well, if the RIV-ER WAS WHIS - KEY, AND I WAS A DIV - IN' DUCK.
Well, I COULD A HAD A RE - LI - GION, THIS BAD OLD THING IN - STEAD.

WELL, I WOULD DIVE TO THE BOT-TOM,
WELL, NOW WHIS-KEY AND WOM-EN

1. | 2.

NEV - ER WOULD I COME UP. 5. WELL, I
WOULD NOT LET ME PRAY.

Turn on Your Love Light

Words and Music by Don Robey and Joe Scott

🎼 C Version

🎷: C Version

You Can't Judge A Book By The Cover

Written by Willie Dixon

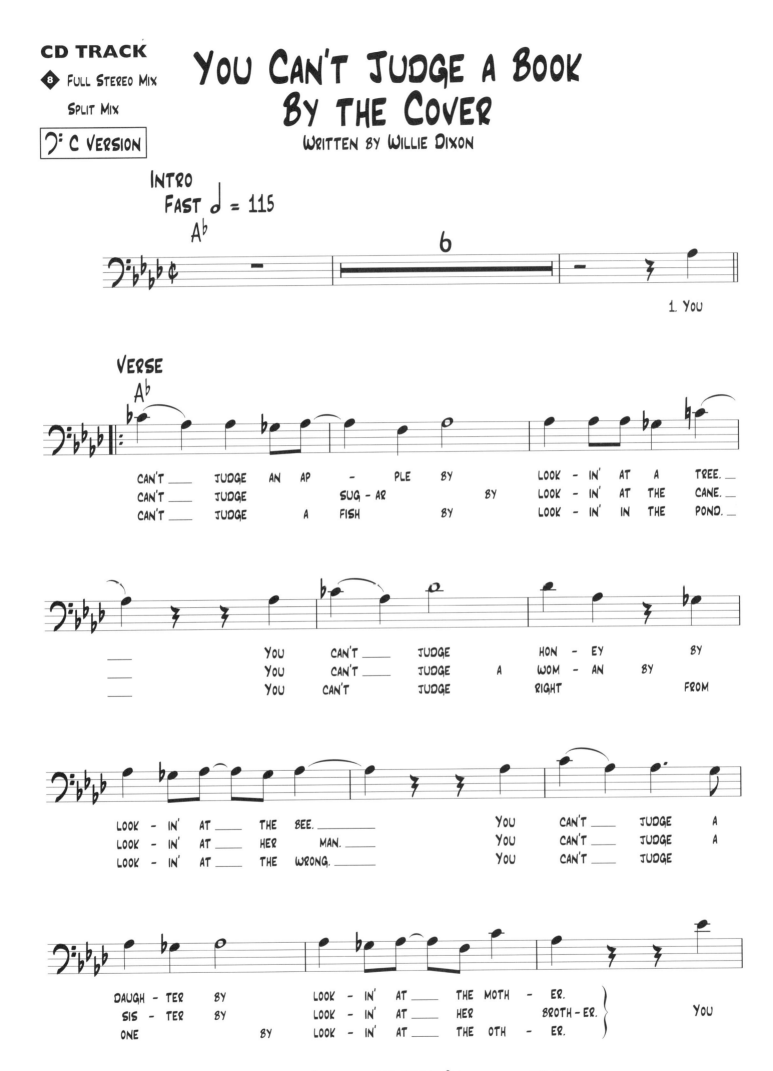

INTRO
Fast ♩ = 115

1. You

VERSE

CAN'T ____ JUDGE AN AP ___ PLE BY LOOK - IN' AT A TREE. ____
CAN'T ____ JUDGE SUG - AR BY LOOK - IN' AT THE CANE. ____
CAN'T ____ JUDGE A FISH BY LOOK - IN' IN THE POND. ____

____ YOU CAN'T ____ JUDGE HON - EY BY
____ YOU CAN'T ____ JUDGE A WOM - AN BY
____ YOU CAN'T JUDGE RIGHT FROM

LOOK - IN' AT ____ THE BEE. _____ YOU CAN'T ____ JUDGE A
LOOK - IN' AT ____ HER MAN. _____ YOU CAN'T ____ JUDGE A
LOOK - IN' AT ____ THE WRONG. _____ YOU CAN'T ____ JUDGE

DAUGH - TER BY LOOK - IN' AT ____ THE MOTH - ER.
SIS - TER BY LOOK - IN' AT ____ HER BROTH - ER. ⎫ YOU
ONE BY LOOK - IN' AT ____ THE OTH - ER. ⎭

Prices, content, and availability subject to change without notice.

The Best-Selling Jazz Book of All Time Is Now Legal!

SIXTH EDITION

THE REAL BOOK

The Real Books are the most popular jazz books of all time. Since the 1970s, musicians have trusted these volumes to get them through every gig, night after night. The problem is that the books were illegally produced and distributed, without any regard to copyright law, or royalties paid to the composers who created these musical masterpieces.

Hal Leonard is very proud to present the first legitimate and legal editions of these books ever produced. You won't even notice the difference, other than all the notorious errors being fixed: the covers and typeface look the same, the song lists are nearly identical, and the price for our edition is even cheaper than the originals!

Every conscientious musician will appreciate that these books are now produced accurately and ethically, benefitting the songwriters that we owe for some of the greatest tunes of all time!

VOLUME 1
00240221	C Edition	$32.50
00240224	B♭ Edition	$32.50
00240225	E♭ Edition	$32.50
00240226	Bass Clef Edition	$32.50
00240292	C Edition 6 x 9	$27.95
00451087	C Edition on CD-ROM	$25.00
00240302	A-D Play-Along CDs	$24.99
00240303	E-J Play-Along CDs	$24.95
00240304	L-R Play-Along CDs	$24.95
00240305	S-Z Play-Along CDs	$24.99

VOLUME 2
00240222	C Edition	$32.50
00240227	B♭ Edition	$32.50
00240228	E♭ Edition	$32.50
00240229	Bass Clef Edition	$32.50
00240293	C Edition 6 x 9	$27.95
00240351	A-D Play-Along CDs	$24.99
00240352	E-I Play-Along CDs	$24.99
00240353	J-R Play-Along CDs	$24.99
00240354	S-Z Play-Along CDs	$24.99

VOLUME 3
00240233	C Edition	$32.50
00240284	B♭ Edition	$32.50
00240285	E♭ Edition	$32.50
00240286	Bass Clef Edition	$32.50

VOLUME 4
00240296	C Edition	$29.99
00103349	E♭ Edition	$32.50

VOLUME 5
00240349	C Edition	$32.50

Also available:
00240264	The Real Blues Book	$34.99
00310910	The Real Bluegrass Book	$29.99
00240137	Miles Davis Real Book	$19.95
00240355	The Real Dixieland Book	$29.99
00240235	The Duke Ellington Real Book	$19.99
00240358	The Charlie Parker Real Book	$19.99
00240331	The Bud Powell Real Book	$19.99
00240313	The Real Rock Book	$32.50
00240323	The Real Rock Book – Vol. 2	$39.95
00240359	The Real Tab Book – Vol. 1	$32.50
00240317	The Real Worship Book	$29.99

THE REAL CHRISTMAS BOOK
00240306	C Edition	$25.00
00240345	B♭ Edition	$25.00
00240346	E♭ Edition	$25.00
00240347	Bass Clef Edition	$25.00
00240431	A-G Play-Along CDs	$24.99
00240432	H-M Play-Along CDs	$24.99
00240433	N-Y Play-Along CDs	$24.99

THE REAL VOCAL BOOK
00240230	Volume 1 High Voice	$32.50
00240307	Volume 1 Low Voice	$32.50
00240231	Volume 2 High Voice	$32.50
00240308	Volume 2 Low Voice	$29.95
00240391	Volume 3 High Voice	$29.99
00240392	Volume 3 Low Voice	$29.99

THE REAL BOOK – STAFF PAPER
00240327		$9.95

HOW TO PLAY FROM A REAL BOOK
FOR ALL MUSICIANS
by Robert Rawlins
00312097	$14.99

Complete song lists online at www.halleonard.com
Prices and availability subject to change without notice.

HAL•LEONARD® CORPORATION
7777 W. BLUEMOUND RD. P.O. BOX 13819 MILWAUKEE, WI 53213

1012

66. A CHARLIE BROWN CHRISTMAS
00843067......................................$16.99

67. CHICK COREA
00843068......................................$15.95

68. CHARLES MINGUS
00843069......................................$16.95

69. CLASSIC JAZZ
00843071......................................$15.99

70. THE DOORS
00843072......................................$14.95

71. COLE PORTER CLASSICS
00843073......................................$14.95

72. CLASSIC JAZZ BALLADS
00843074......................................$15.99

73. JAZZ/BLUES
00843075......................................$14.95

74. BEST JAZZ CLASSICS
00843076......................................$15.99

75. PAUL DESMOND
00843077......................................$15.99

76. BROADWAY JAZZ BALLADS
00843078......................................$15.99

77. JAZZ ON BROADWAY
00843079......................................$15.99

78. STEELY DAN
00843070......................................$15.99

79. MILES DAVIS CLASSICS
00843081......................................$15.99

80. JIMI HENDRIX
00843083......................................$16.99

81. FRANK SINATRA – CLASSICS
00843084......................................$15.99

82. FRANK SINATRA – STANDARDS
00843085......................................$15.99

83. ANDREW LLOYD WEBBER
00843104......................................$14.95

84. BOSSA NOVA CLASSICS
00843105......................................$14.95

85. MOTOWN HITS
00843109......................................$14.95

86. BENNY GOODMAN
00843110......................................$15.99

87. DIXIELAND
00843111......................................$14.95

88. DUKE ELLINGTON FAVORITES
00843112......................................$14.95

89. IRVING BERLIN FAVORITES
00843113......................................$14.95

90. THELONIOUS MONK CLASSICS
00841262......................................$16.99

91. THELONIOUS MONK FAVORITES
00841263......................................$16.99

92. LEONARD BERNSTEIN
00450134......................................$15.99

93. DISNEY FAVORITES
00843142......................................$14.99

94. RAY
00843143......................................$14.99

95. JAZZ AT THE LOUNGE
00843144......................................$14.99

96. LATIN JAZZ STANDARDS
00843145......................................$15.99

97. MAYBE I'M AMAZED*
00843148......................................$15.99

98. DAVE FRISHBERG
00843149......................................$15.99

99. SWINGING STANDARDS
00843150......................................$14.99

100. LOUIS ARMSTRONG
00740423......................................$16.99

101. BUD POWELL
00843152......................................$14.99

102. JAZZ POP
00843153......................................$15.99

103. ON GREEN DOLPHIN STREET & OTHER JAZZ CLASSICS
00843154......................................$14.99

104. ELTON JOHN
00843155......................................$14.99

105. SOULFUL JAZZ
00843151......................................$15.99

106. SLO' JAZZ
00843117......................................$14.99

107. MOTOWN CLASSICS
00843116......................................$14.99

108. JAZZ WALTZ
00843159......................................$15.99

109. OSCAR PETERSON
00843160......................................$16.99

110. JUST STANDARDS
00843161......................................$15.99

111. COOL CHRISTMAS
00843162......................................$15.99

112. PAQUITO D'RIVERA – LATIN JAZZ*
48020662......................................$16.99

113. PAQUITO D'RIVERA – BRAZILIAN JAZZ*
48020663......................................$19.99

114. MODERN JAZZ QUARTET FAVORITES
00843163......................................$15.99

115. THE SOUND OF MUSIC
00843164......................................$15.99

116. JACO PASTORIUS
00843165......................................$15.99

117. ANTONIO CARLOS JOBIM – MORE HITS
00843166......................................$15.99

118. BIG JAZZ STANDARDS COLLECTION
00843167......................................$27.50

119. JELLY ROLL MORTON
00843168......................................$15.99

120. J.S. BACH
00843169......................................$15.99

121. DJANGO REINHARDT
00843170......................................$15.99

122. PAUL SIMON
00843182......................................$16.99

123. BACHARACH & DAVID
00843185......................................$15.99

124. JAZZ-ROCK HORN HITS
00843186......................................$15.99

126. COUNT BASIE CLASSICS
00843157......................................$15.99

127. CHUCK MANGIONE
00843188......................................$15.99

128. VOCAL STANDARDS (LOW VOICE)
00843189......................................$15.99

129. VOCAL STANDARDS (HIGH VOICE)
00843190......................................$15.99

130. VOCAL JAZZ (LOW VOICE)
00843191......................................$15.99

131. VOCAL JAZZ (HIGH VOICE)
00843192......................................$15.99

132. STAN GETZ ESSENTIALS
00843193......................................$15.99

133. STAN GETZ FAVORITES
00843194......................................$15.99

134. NURSERY RHYMES*
00843196......................................$17.99

135. JEFF BECK
00843197......................................$15.99

136. NAT ADDERLEY
00843198......................................$15.99

137. WES MONTGOMERY
00843199......................................$15.99

138. FREDDIE HUBBARD
00843200......................................$15.99

139. JULIAN "CANNONBALL" ADDERLEY
00843201......................................$15.99

140. JOE ZAWINUL
00843202......................................$15.99

141. BILL EVANS STANDARDS
00843156......................................$15.99

142. CHARLIE PARKER GEMS
00843222......................................$15.99

143. JUST THE BLUES
00843223......................................$15.99

144. LEE MORGAN
00843229......................................$15.99

145. COUNTRY STANDARDS
00843230......................................$15.99

146. RAMSEY LEWIS
00843231......................................$15.99

147. SAMBA
00843232......................................$15.99

150. JAZZ IMPROV BASICS
00843195......................................$19.99

151. MODERN JAZZ QUARTET CLASSICS
00843209......................................$15.99

152. J.J. JOHNSON
00843210......................................$15.99

154. HENRY MANCINI
00843213......................................$14.99

155. SMOOTH JAZZ CLASSICS
00843215......................................$15.99

156. THELONIOUS MONK – EARLY GEMS
00843216......................................$15.99

157. HYMNS
00843217......................................$15.99

158. JAZZ COVERS ROCK
00843219......................................$15.99

159. MOZART
00843220......................................$15.99

160. GEORGE SHEARING
14041531......................................$16.99

161. DAVE BRUBECK
14041556......................................$16.99

162. BIG CHRISTMAS COLLECTION
00843221......................................$24.99

164. HERB ALPERT
14041775......................................$16.99

*These CDs do not include split tracks.

1012

ARTIST TRANSCRIPTIONS

Artist Transcriptions are authentic, note-for-note transcriptions of today's hottest artists in jazz, pop and rock. These outstanding, accurate arrangements are in an easy-to-read format which includes all essential lines. Artist Transcriptions can be used to perform, sequence or for reference.

CLARINET
00672423	Buddy De Franco Collection	$19.95

FLUTE
00672379	Eric Dolphy Collection	$19.95
00672582	The Very Best of James Galway	$16.99
00672372	James Moody Collection – Sax and Flute	$19.95
00660108	James Newton – Improvising Flute	$14.95

GUITAR & BASS
00660113	The Guitar Style of George Benson	$14.95
00699072	Guitar Book of Pierre Bensusan	$29.95
00672331	Ron Carter – Acoustic Bass	$16.95
00672307	Stanley Clarke Collection	$19.95
00660115	Al Di Meola – Friday Night in San Francisco	$14.95
00604043	Al Di Meola – Music, Words, Pictures	$14.95
00672574	Al Di Meola – Pursuit of Radical Rhapsody	$22.99
00673245	Jazz Style of Tal Farlow	$19.95
00672359	Bela Fleck and the Flecktones	$18.95
00699389	Jim Hall – Jazz Guitar Environments	$19.95
00699306	Jim Hall – Exploring Jazz Guitar	$19.95
00604049	Allan Holdsworth – Reaching for the Uncommon Chord	$14.95
00699215	Leo Kottke – Eight Songs	$14.95
00675536	Wes Montgomery – Guitar Transcriptions	$17.95
00672353	Joe Pass Collection	$18.95
00673216	John Patitucci	$16.95
00027083	Django Reinhardt Antholog	$14.95
00026711	Genius of Django Reinhardt	$10.95
00672374	Johnny Smith Guitar Solos	$19.99
00672320	Mark Whitfield	$19.95

PIANO & KEYBOARD
00672338	Monty Alexander Collection	$19.95
00672487	Monty Alexander Plays Standards	$19.95
00672520	Count Basie Collection	$19.95
00672439	Cyrus Chestnut Collection	$19.95
00672300	Chick Corea – Paint the World	$12.95
00672537	Bill Evans at Town Hall	$16.95
00672548	The Mastery of Bill Evans	$12.95
00672425	Bill Evans – Piano Interpretations	$19.95
00672365	Bill Evans – Piano Standards	$19.95
00672510	Bill Evans Trio – Vol. 1: 1959-1961	$24.95
00672511	Bill Evans Trio – Vol. 2: 1962-1965	$24.95
00672512	Bill Evans Trio – Vol. 3: 1968-1974	$24.95
00672513	Bill Evans Trio – Vol. 4: 1979-1980	$24.95
00672381	Tommy Flanagan Collection	$24.99
00672492	Benny Goodman Collection	$16.95
00672486	Vince Guaraldi Collection	$19.95
00672419	Herbie Hancock Collection	$19.95
00672438	Hampton Hawes	$19.95
00672322	Ahmad Jamal Collection	$22.95
00672564	Best of Jeff Lorber	$17.99
00672476	Brad Mehldau Collection	$19.99
00672388	Best of Thelonious Monk	$19.95

00672389	Thelonious Monk Collection	$19.95
00672390	Thelonious Monk Plays Jazz Standards – Volume 1	$19.95
00672391	Thelonious Monk Plays Jazz Standards – Volume 2	$19.95
00672433	Jelly Roll Morton – The Piano Rolls	$12.95
00672553	Charlie Parker for Piano	$19.95
00672542	Oscar Peterson – Jazz Piano Solos	$16.95
00672562	Oscar Peterson – A Jazz Portrait of Frank Sinatra	$19.95
00672544	Oscar Peterson – Originals	$9.95
00672532	Oscar Peterson – Plays Broadway	$19.95
00672531	Oscar Peterson – Plays Duke Ellington	$19.95
00672563	Oscar Peterson – A Royal Wedding Suite	$19.99
00672533	Oscar Peterson – Trios	$24.95
00672543	Oscar Peterson Trio – Canadiana Suite	$10.99
00672534	Very Best of Oscar Peterson	$22.95
00672371	Bud Powell Classics	$19.95
00672376	Bud Powell Collection	$19.95
00672437	André Previn Collection	$19.95
00672507	Gonzalo Rubalcaba Collection	$19.95
00672303	Horace Silver Collection	$19.95
00672316	Art Tatum Collection	$22.95
00672355	Art Tatum Solo Book	$19.95
00672357	Billy Taylor Collection	$24.95
00673215	McCoy Tyner	$16.95
00672321	Cedar Walton Collection	$19.95
00672519	Kenny Werner Collection	$19.95
00672434	Teddy Wilson Collection	$19.95

SAXOPHONE
00672566	The Mindi Abair Collection	$14.99
00673244	Julian "Cannonball" Adderley Collection	$19.95
00673237	Michael Brecker	$19.95
00672429	Michael Brecker Collection	$19.95
00672315	Benny Carter Plays Standards	$22.95
00672314	Benny Carter Collection	$22.95
00672394	James Carter Collection	$19.95
00672349	John Coltrane Plays Giant Steps	$19.95
00672529	John Coltrane – Giant Steps	$14.99
00672494	John Coltrane – A Love Supreme	$14.95
00307393	John Coltrane – Omnibook: C Instruments	$19.99
00307391	John Coltrane – Omnibook: B-flat Instruments	$19.99
00307392	John Coltrane – Omnibook: E-flat Instruments	$19.99
00307394	John Coltrane – Omnibook: Bass Clef Instruments	$19.99
00672493	John Coltrane Plays "Coltrane Changes"	$19.95
00672453	John Coltrane Plays Standards	$19.95
00673233	John Coltrane Solos	$22.95
00672328	Paul Desmond Collection	$19.95
00672379	Eric Dolphy Collection	$19.95
00672530	Kenny Garrett Collection	$19.95

00699375	Stan Getz	$19.95
00672377	Stan Getz – Bossa Novas	$19.95
00672375	Stan Getz – Standards	$18.95
00673254	Great Tenor Sax Solos	$18.95
00672523	Coleman Hawkins Collection	$19.95
00673252	Joe Henderson – Selections from "Lush Life" & "So Near So Far"	$19.95
00672330	Best of Joe Henderson	$22.95
00672350	Tenor Saxophone Standards	$18.95
00673239	Best of Kenny G	$19.95
00673229	Kenny G – Breathless	$19.95
00672462	Kenny G – Classics in the Key of G	$19.95
00672485	Kenny G – Faith: A Holiday Album	$14.95
00672373	Kenny G – The Moment	$19.95
00672326	Joe Lovano Collection	$19.95
00672498	Jackie McLean Collection	$19.95
00672372	James Moody Collection – Sax and Flute	$19.95
00672416	Frank Morgan Collection	$19.95
00672539	Gerry Mulligan Collection	$19.95
00672352	Charlie Parker Collection	$19.95
00672561	Best of Sonny Rollins	$19.95
00672444	Sonny Rollins Collection	$19.95
00102751	Sonny Rollins with the Modern Jazz Quartet	$17.99
00675000	David Sanborn Collection	$17.95
00672528	Bud Shank Collection	$19.95
00672491	New Best of Wayne Shorter	$19.95
00672550	The Sonny Stitt Collection	$19.95
00672350	Tenor Saxophone Standards	$18.95
00672567	The Best of Kim Waters	$17.99
00672524	Lester Young Collection	$19.95

TROMBONE
00672332	J.J. Johnson Collection	$19.95
00672489	Steve Turré Collection	$19.99

TRUMPET
00672557	Herb Alpert Collection	$14.99
00672480	Louis Armstrong Collection	$17.95
00672481	Louis Armstrong Plays Standards	$17.95
00672435	Chet Baker Collection	$19.95
00672556	Best of Chris Botti	$19.95
00672448	Miles Davis – Originals, Vol. 1	$19.95
00672451	Miles Davis – Originals, Vol. 2	$19.95
00672450	Miles Davis – Standards, Vol. 1	$19.95
00672449	Miles Davis – Standards, Vol. 2	$19.95
00672479	Dizzy Gillespie Collection	$19.95
00673214	Freddie Hubbard	$14.95
00672382	Tom Harrell – Jazz Trumpet	$19.95
00672363	Jazz Trumpet Solos	$9.95
00672506	Chuck Mangione Collection	$19.95
00672525	Arturo Sandoval – Trumpet Evolution	$19.95

HAL•LEONARD® CORPORATION
7777 W. BLUEMOUND RD. P.O. BOX 13819 MILWAUKEE, WI 53213

Visit our web site for a complete listing of our titles with songlists at
www.halleonard.com

0113

Prices and availability subject to change without notice.